THE SHURLEY METHOD

Literature Selections

LEVEL 6

Brenda Shurley

Shurley Instructional Materials, Inc., Cabot, Arkansas

Acknowledgements

Grateful acknowledgement is due the following publishers, authors, and other holders of copyright material for the permission to use selections from their publications.

THE ESTATE OF EDGAR LEE MASTERS: "Seth Compton," reprinted from *Spoon River Anthology*, published by The Macmillan Company. Reprinted with permission of Hilary Masters.

HARDING STEDLER: "Soulstring on the South Wind," from *Where Downsides Are Upsides and Outsides Are In*, copyright © 1990. Reprinted with permission of the author.

TRUSTEES OF AMHERST COLLEGE: "I'm Nobody," reprinted by permission of the publishers and the Trustees of Amherst College from *The Poems of Emily Dickinson*, Thomas H. Johnson, ed. Cambridge, MASS.: The Belknap Press of Harvard University Press, Copyright © 1951, 1955, 1979, 1983 by the President and Fellows of Harvard College.

Bob Wilson, Ph.D.

I would like to personally thank Bob Wilson for all the hard work he put forth in helping to create this series. He spent countless hours in search of just the right works to be included in the Literature Selections. I could not have gotten this publication ready without him. Thank you, Bob, for your happy spirit while we were trying to meet deadlines. All your efforts are truly appreciated.

We also gratefully thank the following people for their help and support in the preparation of this book:

Ardean Coffman	Gil Strackbein	Kim Spicher-Shurley
Keith Covington	Billy Shurley, Sr.	Andrea Shurley-Turkia
Shurley Method Staff	Billy Ray Shurley, Jr.	Jani-Petri Rainer Turkia

First Edition
ISBN 1-881940-99-3 (Level 6 Literature Selections)

♦ For additional information or to place an order, write to Shurley Instructional Materials, Inc., 366 SIM Drive, Cabot, AR 72023, or call 1-800-566-2966.

INTRODUCTION

Welcome to *The Shurley Method: Literature Selections* for Level 6. It is with much excitement and enthusiasm that we provide today's youth with an early exposure to selections of contemporary and non-contemporary literature alike. The contemporary selections are subtitled *Literature of the New Millennium: Contemporary Authors*, and the non-contemporary selections are subtitled *Beacons from the Past: Lights on Literature.*

The contemporary selections contained in this collection have been written by a diverse group of authors for the *New Millennium*, the 21st century. The poems and prose pieces were selected from hundreds of entries that were submitted for consideration. The authors come from varied backgrounds and from various parts of the country. Some have published extensively; others have written primarily for their own personal gratification.

The topics of the authors of the *New Millennium* are contemporary as well. To read and analyze these selections, students will be able to relate to subject matter of their time.

That students might relate to the authors, a biographical sketch accompanies each selection. And to help them more fully understand the poems and prose selections, a series of discussion questions follows each story and poem.

The non-contemporary selections contained in this collection have been chosen to expose students to different authors from the past that they may not have encountered otherwise. To make this study of non-contemporary literature more pleasurable for students, the editors of *Beacons from the Past* have designed a series of questions to actively engage students in the study of selected poems. The questions are designed to engage students in writing and/or speaking, with the poems serving as either models or stepping-stones for student writing.

Many of the shorter selections can be taught in one class period. However, many of the longer pieces may require two or three days' study—some, even a full week. There is nothing sacred about "a title a day." Some selections invite more discussion than others. Some activities—especially writing-related exercises—will require more than one day to complete. There is much to be said for being thorough and engaging students with each selection they study. Allowing them time to enjoy and appreciate works of literature can be as important as giving them an understanding of it.

It is our fondest hope that students will find *The Shurley Method: Literature Selections* compelling and that they will be engaged from the outset with the characters in each piece. By utilizing the discussion questions, we believe that students will develop a discerning eye for detail and that they will be aware of not only what a passage says, but also what it means.

Brenda Shurley

WHAT IS POETRY?

Welcome to the world of artistic writing, sometimes referred to as creative writing. Artistic writing includes many literary **genres**--essays, poems, short stories, plays, etc. A genre is the type of writing a piece of literature is. Of course, there are the broad categories of prose and poetry, but each of these can be divided more specifically. Types of prose include drama, articles, novels, and short stories. Types of poetry include lyric and narrative.

The poem, whether it rhymes or not, is probably the most artistic of all genres. A poem is a delicate juggling act of rhythms, figurative language, and sometimes rhyme. The poem as an art form is both visual and auditory.

A poem will most often have sections, or divisions, that are identified as either **stanzas** or **strophes**. **Stanzas** are divisions of a rhyming poem, and **strophes** are divisions of a poem that does not rhyme, and may also be known as **free verse**.

A reader, without reading words, can look at a poem and know it is a poem by its appearance on the page. Likewise, a listener can hear a poem read aloud and know it is a poem because it sounds like one.

The earliest poems written in English were ones that rhymed. Even though much modern-day poetry does not rhyme, rhyme is a device that helps to structure a poem and makes it easy to commit the poem to memory.

WHAT IS PROSE?

In the world of artistic writing, **prose** is the form that most creative writing takes on--in the **genres** of essays, articles, short stories, novels, and plays. Rather than **stanzas** and **strophes**, most **prosaic** pieces are divided into **paragraphs**--sometimes with dialogue, sometimes not. Sometimes, the stories are true; sometimes, they are purely fictional. The vast majority of stories, however, are ones rooted in an actual event, but embellished for the sake of the story.

Dialogue is conversation. Two or more characters interact with each other through language. The actual words spoken, contained within quotation marks, make the story more believable and often heighten the intensity of a plot.

So, **dialogue** is what the characters tell you; **narration** is what the author tells you. And it typically takes both to make a good story.

Literature of the New Millennium:

Contemporary Authors

Poetry

"Hoops"
"No Right Words"
"Noah's Wife"
"School"
"Soulstring on the South Wind"
"To My Child"

Prose

"The Seasons"

About the Student Author: Nathan Workman is the 18 year-old son of Ernie and Ellen Workman and is currently a senior at Stilwell High School, in Stilwell, Oklahoma. Next year, he will be attending the University of Arkansas in Fayetteville, where he will study Communications. Writing started as a chore for Workman, but it soon became his favorite pastime. He discovered that he had a talent for writing. Workman and his grandmother, Jewell Williams, have had their poetry published. His mother writes a weekly column for the local newspaper. Workman wrote this particular selection while he was in the seventh grade.

Hoops

I got the ball
Nothin' to fear
What's gonna stop me?
The hoop is near

I take it to the hole
I fake to my left
Fade-away falls
The crowd screams Yes!

Defense! Defense!
Is the new cry
The shot goes up
And so do I

The shot is deflected
The break is on
I take a look behind me
The defense is gone

I go behind the back
Take a spin or two
I go up—
And the ball goes through

Slammin'
Jammin'
Shootin' the trey
Moves I'll need for a rainy day

--Nathan Workman

Discussion Ideas for “Hoops”

Listen to the poem read aloud the first time for enjoyment. Then, read and discuss the information that is written about the author of the poem. After that, read the poem silently as the poem is read aloud for the second time. After the second reading, you should be able to talk about the discussion ideas listed below.

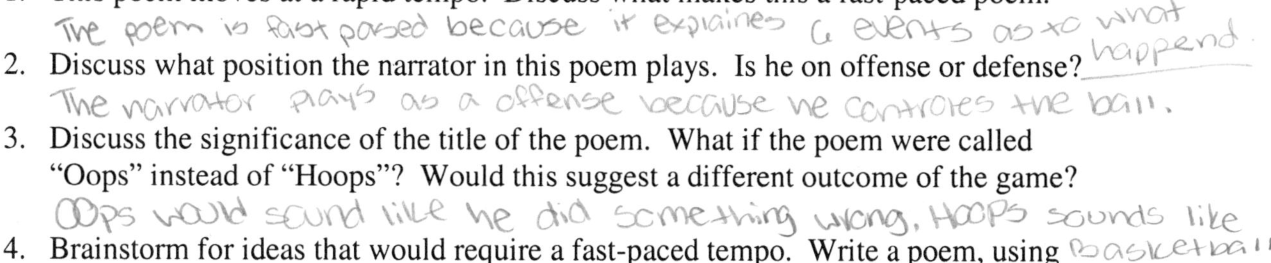

1. This poem moves at a rapid tempo. Discuss what makes this a fast-paced poem.
   The poem is fast posed because it explaines 6 events as to what happend.
2. Discuss what position the narrator in this poem plays. Is he on offense or defense?
   The narrator plays as a offense because he controles the ball.
3. Discuss the significance of the title of the poem. What if the poem were called “Oops” instead of “Hoops”? Would this suggest a different outcome of the game?
   OOps would sound like he did something wrong. HOOPS sounds like basketball.
4. Brainstorm for ideas that would require a fast-paced tempo. Write a poem, using some of the ideas gathered while brainstorming. Share your poem with others.

5. Keep a writer’s notebook, either on paper or on the computer, to record impromptu or assigned poems and stories. Proofread for errors and make sure all spelling is correct by the use of a dictionary, a computer spell-check, etc., before handing in a final paper.

About the Student Author: Jenifer Ransom is a graduate of Conway High School in Arkansas. She is currently seeking a Computer Information Systems degree from Southeast College of Technology in Conway. She has always enjoyed writing poetry, and love poems are her favorites. She wrote this love poem when she was fourteen years old.

No Right Words

Why do I love you so?
Could it be the way
  you look at me?
Or could it be
  the things you say?
If I could only
  find the right words
  to tell you how I feel,
  then, maybe, I too would know
  the reason why
  I love you so.

--Jenifer D. Ransom

Discussion Ideas for "No Right Words"

Listen to the poem read aloud the first time for enjoyment. Then, read and discuss the information that is written about the author of the poem. After that, read the poem silently as the poem is read aloud for the second time. After the second reading, you should be able to talk about the discussion ideas listed below.

1. Discuss how you know that the narrator loves the other person intensely.
   I know because of the narrator expresses his feeling for the other person
2. Discuss how the first and last lines contribute to the design of the poem.
   At first he's not sure why he loves that person, then, at the end, he found out why.
3. Write a poem of love from a boy's point of view. Share your poem with others.
4. Write a poem of love from a girl's point of view. Share your poem with others.

About the Student Author: Born in Dallas, Texas, Ashley Spicer now lives in Jennings, Louisiana, where she is a high school sophomore. Not only does Spicer write, she has also been in numerous musical productions. While attending the Governor's Program for Gifted Children in Lake Charles during the summer of 1999, she wrote this poem.

Noah's Wife

Sleeping is impossible.
The torrents of rain
pound persistently
on the wooden roof
like fire and brimstone
cast down from Heaven.

Noah tells me to have faith…
that this storm won't last.
But the animals still bray and bleat
for food as though they had had none for months,
and the waves still beat
at the ark's hull.

At night doubts slip into
my mind like the water seeping
between these boards.

I long for warm sun on my neck
and for dry air in my hair…
but I have not seen
sunlight for days,
and the stale air here
sticks to my skin.

And all the while the ark rocks
back and forth
back and forth.

--Ashley Spicer

Discussion Ideas for "Noah's Wife"

Listen to the poem read aloud the first time for enjoyment. Then, read and discuss the information that is written about the author of the poem. After that, read the poem silently as the poem is read aloud for the second time. After the second reading, you should be able to talk about the discussion ideas listed below.

1. This poem was inspired by a person who played a very important role in the story of Noah's Ark but never received any recognition for it. Think of some other unsung heroes you may have noticed in a story and give examples of why they are important. (Example: "The mirror" in *Snow White and the Seven Dwarfs*.)

2. In "Noah's Wife," the author uses different techniques to make her readers feel as though they were actually on the ark. One example is the repetition used in the last strophe, where the author writes "back and forth" twice to give the effect of the swaying of the ark. See if you can come up with some examples of other techniques used.

3. Choose an author you would like to know more about and gather information about that author's works. In order to research your topic, use the library resources or your home resources, which should include any of the following: non-fiction books, encyclopedias, magazine articles, CD-ROM references, and on-line information services.

4. Collaborate with your teacher and invite a guest writer to your class. After the writer's presentation, ask pertinent questions about his/her works. You might also discuss how the writer chooses a topic and an audience for his/her works. Write a thank-you note to thank the speaker for coming. Be sure to mention the part of the presentation you enjoyed the most. Write your thank-you note neatly and edit it carefully for mistakes, including spelling errors. Give your thank-you note to your teacher to send to the guest speaker.

About the Author: Ellwood Grenvall was born and raised in Minnesota. An only child, he attended college at the University of Minnesota before joining the United States Navy. Grenvall served his country in World War II in the South Pacific. Grenvall displayed an early gift for writing that his children and grandchildren have inherited. He was an electrician by trade, but wrote numerous poems while in high school. After his death, his daughter came across many of his works. This is one of his earlier poems that was written in 1927 at the age of seventeen.

School

School is an institution of grief,
some of the pupils say.
I don't know, though it might be,
but I can't see it that way.

In school you have your parties,
as all of you must know.
At them, you can have more fun
than at any picture show.

Of course, you have your studies,
which you should never shirk.
But some pupils are neglectful
and do not care to work.

And again, you cannot whisper;
"It's against the rules", they say.
But I feel sure in saying
it's one they don't obey.

Chewing gum is another thing
they will not let you do,
but so many pupils enjoy it.
and I think I do, too.

--Ellwood Grenvall

Discussion Ideas for "School"

Listen to the poem read aloud the first time for enjoyment. Then, read and discuss the information that is written about the author of the poem. After that, read the poem silently as the poem is read aloud for the second time. After the second reading, you should be able to talk about the discussion ideas listed below.

1. Do your think the narrator of this poem really disliked school? Why or why not?

2. Select and discuss two examples of the author's sense of humor.

3. What are some student behaviors that are against the rules? How do they compare to today's school rules?

4. Interview your parents, grandparents, neighbors, or friends to find out what schools were like during their youth. Then, write a story about what it would be like for you to travel back in time and go to school during their time period.

5. Write a second story about what it would be like to have your grandparents travel forward in time and go to school in the present.

About the Author: Founder and director of the Little Smokies of Ohio Fall Poetry Workshop, held annually at Murphin Ridge Inn in Amish country of Southern Ohio, Harding Stedler is a retired Professor of English. Currently, he serves as secretary of the Poets' Roundtable of Arkansas and has four published books of poems. His most recent collection is *Where Downsides Are Upsides and Outsides Are In.*

Soulstring on the South Wind

South winds change dormant seasons,
drive winter into hiding.
South winds calibrate my heartbeat.

Long a victim of jet stream's arctic darkness,
and back against the north wind,
I welcome new beginnings.

At last, I ride the air waves
on chorales of feathered wing,
singing freedom's songs.

I crack the egg of dawn
and, from that precipice,
pierce the world with hope.

I tune my soulstring on the south wind
and make rhapsodies that stir
green-leafed dancers, waiting.

Call me fledgling,
with a burgeoning dream to fly.
Tomorrow is my mate.

--Harding Stedler

Discussion Ideas for "Soulstring on the South Wind"

Listen to the poem read aloud the first time for enjoyment. Then, read and discuss the information that is written about the author of the poem. After that, read the poem silently as the poem is read aloud for the second time. After the second reading, you should be able to talk about the discussion ideas listed below.

1. Why is "Tomorrow…my mate"?
2. The poem is one of metamorphosis. Discuss how the narrator is transformed and by what.
3. What is strophe 5 telling you about the kinship of the writer with nature?
4. In strophe 2, why is the narrator "back against the north wind"?
5. Discuss how you would define a "soulstring."
6. Choose a poem or story to read aloud. By presenting poems or stories orally, you can gain some insight into how to write them effectively. Discuss the audience and the purpose for which the poem or story was written. Tell whether you liked or disliked the poem or story and why.
7. Winds of change are blowing all over the country and in other nations. Look for current events in newspapers or magazines that tell about these changes. Make a collage from the articles and pictures that help you tell the story about changes throughout the world.
8. Write a summary of the things you have learned as you put your collage together.

About the Author: Judith Spicher is originally from Illinois. She began writing poetry while in junior high school. In high school, two of her poems were published in the *National High School Anthology.* She has worked in various jobs over the years: as a telephone operator and supervisor, office supervisor, operating-room technician, education counselor, wife, and mother. She has traveled extensively both in the United States and Europe. She found time to earn a Bachelor of Arts degree in Behavioral Science from California Baptist College and a Master of Education degree in Counseling from Boston University. She is currently retired and living in Arkansas.

To My Child

Joy and Laughter, Sorrow and Tears,
These we shared throughout the Years.
Now you leave these years behind,
Not knowing what you'll seek and find.

As you stretch your wings and fly,
New adventures you will try.
I watch you go with Joy and Sorrow,
And wish for you all bright tomorrows.

Once more my daily prayer, I pray:
May God protect you on your way.

Love Always,

Mom

--Judith Spicher

Discussion Ideas for "To My Child"

Listen to the poem read aloud the first time for enjoyment. Then, read and discuss the information that is written about the author of the poem. After that, read the poem silently as the poem is read aloud for the second time. After the second reading, you should be able to talk about the discussion ideas listed below.

1. There are many words that appear capitalized in this poem that are not normally capitalized. Discuss your ideas about why these words are capitalized.

2. Discuss what emotions the narrator must be feeling about the impeding separation that comes with a child's becoming an adult and leaving home.

3. Discuss why this particular piece might be called a letter poem.

4. A personal letter is a type of expressive writing. Think about a person who has meant a lot to you through the years. It could be a good friend, a family member, a teacher, a relative, etc.

   Write a letter to that person to express what he/she means to you. Then, turn thc feelings you have written in the letter into a poem. You might want to do the poem as an activity in small groups to get input from your peers. If possible, type your letter and poem on the computer and use the spell-check before printing.

   Finally, read your letter and your poem. How do they compare? Which do you like the best? Which was easier? Which copy would you want to send to the person you wrote about?

5. Explore the idea of providing a "literary box" in the classroom for you to contribute written ideas, feelings, or opinions in the form of poetry or prose.

About the Author: As author of *The Shurley Method: English Made Easy*, and as owner of Shurley Instructional Materials, Inc., Brenda Shurley brings a wealth of teaching experience to her current responsibilities. This operetta was written and directed by her, and staged many times by her students, during her twenty years of classroom teaching.

THE SEASONS

Informer 1: Hi! We are the informers.

Informer 2: Introduction is supposed to introduce our operetta, but we want you to be an INFORMED audience before he gets here.

Informer 3: As Earthlings, I'm sure you know very little about sky people. We are a pretty sunny bunch, and we are super easy to get along with.

Informer 4: We take our jobs very seriously—even tho' we do have a good time while we work!

Informer 1: Now, Earthlings, since you know who we are, we want to give you a little information. An operetta is a play with both singing and speaking parts.

Informer 2: We have some wonderful singers. Sky people have come from all over the universe to take part in our program. You'll see what I mean when our voices fill the air with music!

Informer 3: Shhhh! Don't give it away! By the way, Earthlings, you will dearly love the rough and tough tenderhearted seasons and their friends. We sky people never know what they are going to do next!

Informer 4: Our time is up. Introduction is coming, and we have to go. Be sure to remember that you are now an informed audience. Don't forget what we told you.

All: Bye!

Introduction: Hi, Earthlings! I'm Introduction and these are my helpers. We are introducing the operetta. I'm sure you know that an operetta is a play with both singing and speaking parts because the informers have already been here! They love their job of informing, and they have done their job well-—you are an informed audience!

Helper 1: This operetta is about how the seasons came into being. You will love Spring, Summer, Autumn, and Winter because there is something special about each one.

Helper 2: But did you know that one year the seasons had a big fight? I know it's hard to believe, but they did! You poor Earthlings had a really hard time trying to figure out what was wrong with the weather. We sky people all knew what was wrong. And, now, we want to set the record straight.

Introduction: Today, we are going to show you Earthlings what went wrong and how the seasons came into being as we present: THE SEASONS

Narrator 1: The seasons have been pretty rough lately, just as if they were arguing about when each other should come in. I think they have all gathered on top of a little mountain on Earth to discuss their differences. This is something unusual for them. They think of themselves as being much, much higher than to risk letting themselves be seen by Earthlings. This must have been the only place they could agree on. If that is true, they are really having a bad time.

Narrator 2: Yes, but their old friend, Beep, is going to pay them a visit and try to get things straightened out. That's a funny name for a cloud, isn't it? Oh, well. Ah, here comes Beep now. He has that singing group with him. I declare! That bunch will keep anyone happy! They sing all the time, and that suits Beep just fine!

Narrator 1: Let's go a little closer and see what they are saying.

Beep: Come along with me, everyone. I'm just on my way to see how the different seasons are getting along. They are a grouchy bunch sometimes. But it is good to see old friends when you get a chance. By the way, it is a pretty long way, so why don't we sing some songs to pass the time more quickly?

Songs: "If You're Happy and You Know It"
"S-m-i-l-e"
"Polly Wolly Doodle"
"Yankee Doodle"

Beep: Aah....here we are. Look at them all gathered around in a circle. Oh, no! From the look on their faces, they have been arguing again! Now, all of you stay here, and I will go see what is the matter this time!

Now see here, Spring, Summer, Autumn, and Winter. What is all this arguing about? You know how you upset the Earth when you have petty differences among you. And it just isn't right to make Earthlings suffer because of your foolish whimperings!

Winter (in a grumbling voice):

Now, you see here, Beep. I don't think you should voice your opinion until you have heard MY SIDE! Foolish whimperings, pah! Spring is in such a hurry to get her little paw in on things that she is trying to push me out before I'm ready! Why, everytime I turn my back, she sneaks in and the weather turns warm, and flowers peak out, and the birds start singing, and the whole world is in such an uproar!

Song: "Zip-A-Dee-Doo-Dah"

Winter (with disgust):

Why, I get a headache!

Song: "Plop, Plop, Fizz, Fizz"

Spring (in a sweet little voice):

Why, Mr. Winter, I didn't know you were such an old prune!

Song: "Spoonful of Sugar"

Spring (her voice rising):

Push you out indeed! Why, Beep, do you realize what that old windbag does every time I try to bring a little joy and sunshine into his DREARY old season? He just swells up and makes those poor little Earthlings suffer because of his foolish pride. You had it right Beep, HIS foolish whimperings!

Autumn (in a compromising voice):

Now, now, Spring! You must admit you try to push things a little bit. Winter may seem a little COLD and UNBEARABLE sometimes, but you must understand the burden he bears upon his shoulders!

Summer (in a composed voice):

Boy, Autumn, you sure have room to talk! Why, in just the last few months you were complaining about Winter pushing you around—"trying to get his big nose into your season before his time," you said! Now, what do you say to that?

Beep (getting a little upset):

Now, listen, you four! Why in the world would you argue about who comes when? As great as you all think you are, it makes more sense to argue over who has the best season!

Oh, no! I can't believe I said that! Now, you know I didn't mean it! I think you are ALL great! Spring, Summer, Autumn, and Winter, PLEASE believe me! Don't look like that! I REALLY didn't mean that!

Winter (with his voice rising):

Oh, there is no DOUBT about who has the best season! Why, I win that one, hands down!

Autumn (very firmly):

Now, hold on there, Winter. What do you mean, HANDS DOWN? I'm in the race, too, you know!

Summer (with poise):

I really don't know why you two would even argue the point! Why, anyone with half the sense God gave a goose would not even have to pause before they think of ME as the best season!

Spring (with a toss of her head):

Well, I always thought everyone thought of me as the best season. You traitors, leading me to believe that I had the undisputed right to first place! Why, none of you ever said that I did not! That is, not until now!

<u>Winter (his patience growing thin):</u>

Now, Spring, why should we? We've always thought the same thing—that each of us had the undisputed right of first place. BUT now that it has come up, I'll solve the whole thing! I'll take first place!

<u>Narrator 1</u>: Beep is just beside himself! He thinks that it is all his fault that his good friends have suddenly, and without warning, started a sudden and violent weather change on Earth. All the seasons are showing their powers at once. I have never seen anything like it!

(Fans can be turned on, bits of paper scattered over the audience, thunder in the background. Beat on pans, etc.)

<u>Narrator 2</u>: Beep is now worried about the Earth people. If this isn't stopped soon, how will the Earthlings survive? The seasons are getting more upset by the minute! They are all showing their power with more and more strength! The weather is going crazy on Earth! How much longer can they survive? What is going to happen?

<u>Narrator 1:</u> Beep doesn't know what to do! He just stands there wringing his hands in despair! This can't go on much longer—the Earth WILL NOT survive! All the sky people are afraid to interfere. But, LOOK! There to the edge of the group—a CHILD! He is standing!

<u>Narrator 2</u>: As the child stood, the sky people held their breath! What would the seasons do now? Everyone grew quiet as the child spoke. Even the mighty seasons ceased their fighting. Every ear was waiting to hear what the child would say.

<u>Child (with confidence):</u>

It seems pretty simple to me! Since the only way each of you can be satisfied is by proof, why don't you all present things that you have in your season and judge by that?

<u>Winter (breaking the silence with loud enthusiasm):</u>

I'm DELIGHTED that someone finally came up with that idea! Now, I'll show you just how great I really am! And this fine child here will be the judge! It stands to reason that he is not an ODD brain like some of us here. Why, sometimes, you all remind me of an Earthling—scatterbrained, weak, dependent, superstitious, and just all those traits Earthlings have! Not a good sound mind among you!

Spring (with a twinkle in her eye):

All right, Winter, I think that is enough! I take a fancy to Earthlings myself. In fact, every one of us does. Even YOU! Why, I've heard you blabbering and clucking like an old hen over the Earthlings!

Winter(in a mumbling voice):

You sneak around all the time, don't you, Spring?

Autumn (with authority):

Cut it out, you two! I agree with Winter to let this child be the judge. If anyone should know quality, it is the little ones of our world!

Summer (with confidence):

I should think so! Our little ones are special to all of us. Well, I hate to have to prove myself, but this could turn out to be fun!

Beep (with relief):

Well, since you all finally agree on that one, who is going to be first?

Spring (smiling):

Let Winter. He thinks he is the best! Let him be the first one to show himself up!

Narrator 1: Winter agrees that he should be first. As Winter stands with pride, the whole Earth becomes a beautiful winterland of fun and joy. It is truly a majestic sight. The Earth really has problems when the seasons are beside themselves with anger or pride!

Winter: In my GLORIOUS time of the year, there are sports. Loads upon loads of sports to do. And what joyful event is looked forward to more than my Christmas?

Songs: "Up on the Housetop"
"We Wish You a Merry Christmas"

Winter: Besides all the gaiety and gifts, our Christ was born on my day!

Song: "Joy to the World"

Winter: Then, after Christmas, I have the New Year's Day.

Song: "Auld Lang Syne"

Winter: This way, everyone can make resolutions to be a better person. Then, I have Lincoln's Birthday, Washington's Birthday, and, bless everybody's heart, St. Valentine's Day. What a joyous time, Earthlings giving their hearts away. Then, last but not least, I have St. Patrick's Day.

Song: "St. Patrick's Day"

Winter (confidently):

Now, just see if you can top that, Spring.

Narrator 2: Spring definitely thinks that she can do better than Winter! Now, as Spring stands, the whole Earth becomes awe-struck with the splendor and beauty of rebirth.

Spring: Winter, I'll have to give you some credit; you do have your good points. But you still stretch your time just as long as you can. Why, after you finally leave the scene, I already have a late start. But one of the first things I do is honor all the brave mothers for their outstanding job by having Mother's Day.

Song: "Lullaby and Good-Night"

Spring: I spend most of my season honoring everyone. Why, I honor our brave countrymen by having Memorial Day and Flag Day.

Song: "The Star-Spangled Banner"

Spring: Then, I honor our good fathers by saluting them with Father's Day. Oh, yes, and don't forget Easter!

Song: "In Your Easter Bonnet"

Spring: Besides all this, I renew life. I start things growing. I bring freshness everywhere! Birds sing! The Earthlings love me because they can go fishing and fly their kites and enjoy my not-too-cold, not-too-hot weather.

Song: "Let's Go Fly a Kite"

Spring: Now, just how can anyone top all this?

Narrator 1: Summer will not be defeated. As Summer calmly stands, the whole Earth becomes a delight as the warm and loving arms of Summer brings joy everywhere.

Summer: Spring, I admit you are a sweet little thing, and we couldn't do without you, but I just can't see anyone in first place but me. I have some very important events taking place in my season. Why, we got our independence on my day, and I proudly call it Independence Day.

Song: "My Country 'Tis of Thee"

Summer: I also have Labor Day and V-J Day to my credit.

Song: "The Battle Hymn of the Republic"

Summer: Autumn starts pushing into my season as early as he can, too. But people still love me because they get to doze and laze around under my warm sun.

Song: "In the Good Ole Summer Time"

Summer: I warm the Earth and make things grow to their fullest. Earthlings go swimming, go on picnics, and just enjoy life.

Song: "Skip to My Lou"

Summer: Now, just how can anyone ever top that for first place?

Narrator 2: Autumn is not discouraged. As Autumn confidently stands, the whole Earth becomes a glorious display of radiant beauty.

Autumn: Ah, Summer, I'm afraid you have met your match!

Song: "The Old Gray Mare"

Autumn: I hate to outdo a handsome lass like yourself, but there is just no getting around the fact that I'm the best man for the top job. Why, to start my season with a bang, I give the Earthlings the thrill of their lives by having that greatest of events—Halloween!

Song: "This Old Witch"

Autumn: Why, there is not one of the Earthlings that does not look forward to my season. Then, I pay tribute to every soldier alive by having the great and honorable Veteran's Day.

Song: "When Johnny Comes Marching Home"

Autumn: And what do you think my next great event is? Why, give thanks to our Lord—I have that thankful day I proudly call Thanksgiving Day. Everyone eating and giving thanks that Autumn is here.

Song: "Over the River"

Autumn: And then to end my season before Winter comes nosing in, I have Pearl Harbor Day.

Song: "The Marine's Hymn"

Autumn: None of the Earthlings will forget that! And they will never forget me, Autumn, either!

So, you see, I'm tops. Besides, I turn the country into brilliant colors because I make the trees turn the colors of the rainbow. Now, just who can top me?

Narrator 1: After Autumn gets through speaking, all the seasons are speaking at once, each one trying to claim that he is best. I wonder how they are going to settle this one? It seems as though no one is going to give in.

Narrator 2: Oh, Beep is waving his hands, trying to get their attention!

Beep: Now listen, you guys—oh, and ladies. I thought we were going to let the child judge this. You all agreed, remember?

Narrator 1: At this, all eyes turned to the child, who had been forgotten again. Yes, they were interested in him now!

Narrator 2: How could they have forgotten him? He was going to decide which season was tops, best man, and so on. The child had everyone's attention. All the sky people held their breath. What was going to happen now? All is quiet until Beep breaks the silence.

Beep: Well, what is your decision?

Child: I have heard all sides, and here is what I think is fair:

Twelve months in a row; Use them well and let them go.
Welcome them without a fear; Let them go without a tear.
Twelve months in a year; Greet the passing miracle.
Spring and Summer beautiful; Autumn, Winter, gliding on.
Glorious seasons quickly gone; God's treasures in a row.
Take them, love them, let them go. Twelve months in a row.

Author unknown

Now, as judge, this is my verdict. I decreed that there be three months for Spring, three months for Summer, three months for Autumn, and three months for Winter. In the winter months, Winter will sit as king. He shall be tops. But when Spring comes along, he must step down until his months come again. Then, he can just step up again. The same goes for Summer and Autumn. Each of them may step up when their months come along. But then they must step down and rest and let the next season rule for a while. Why, if one season ruled all the time, he would soon give out!

Winter: And out of the mouth of babes!

Spring: That adoring Child! What a masterbrain!

Summer: I've never heard such good advice!

Autumn: We sky people need more like him up here!

Beep: Yes, we do. By the way, Child, what part of the sky do you belong to?

Child: Oh, none in particular. You see, I live below. I'm an Earthling!

Song: "This Land Is Your Land"

Closing Songs:

"A Teacher"
(Choose any song you would like for the student to sing as a closing song.)

Sing while students take their bows:

"I Love to Go a-Wandering"

--Brenda Shurley

Discussion Ideas for "The Seasons"

Read and discuss the information that is written about the author of the story. After reading the story, discuss the questions that follow. The discussion questions will give you insights into characters and events that you may have missed during your first reading of the story.

1. What is an operetta?

2. Who are the sky people? Discuss how they compare with Earthlings.

3. Discuss why it is appropriate that a child be called to arbitrate the differences among the seasons.

4. Discuss the resolution of the conflict among the seasons.

5. Which season do you like the best? Explain your answer.

6. Divide into small groups and write an operetta. Remember to include songs. After you write and edit your operetta, you are now ready to begin working on a multi-media presentation. You should make use of different types of media: audio, video, photos, related art, and/or computer graphics. Finally, design an invitation to send parents, grandparents, relatives, and friends, inviting them to attend your presentation. (This activity may take several sessions to complete.)

Beacons from the Past:

Lights on Literature

"Annabel Lee"
"I'm Nobody"
"Little Boy Blue"
"A Red, Red Rose"
"The Rhodora"
"Seth Compton"

Annabel Lee

It was many and many a year ago,
In a kingdom by the sea,
That a maiden there lived whom you may know
By the name of Annabel Lee;--
And this maiden she lived with no other thought
Than to love and be loved by me.

She was a child and *I* was a child,
In this kingdom by the sea,
But we loved with a love that was more than love—
I and my Annabel Lee—
With a love that the winged seraphs of Heaven
Coveted her and me.

And this was the reason that, long ago,
In this kingdom by the sea,
A wind blew out of a cloud by night
Chilling my Annabel Lee;
So that her highborn kinsmen came
And bore her away from me,
To shut her up in a sepulchre
In this kingdom by the sea.

The angels, not half so happy in Heaven,
Went envying her and me:--
Yes! that was the reason (as all men know,
In this kingdom by the sea)
That the wind came out of the cloud, chilling
And killing my Annabel Lee.

But our love it was stronger by far than the love
Of those who were older than we—
Of many far wiser than we—
And neither the angels in Heaven above
Nor the demons down under the sea,
Can ever dissever my soul from the soul
Of the beautiful Annabel Lee—

For the moon never beams without bringing me dreams
Of the beautiful Annabel Lee;
And the stars never rise but I see the bright eyes
Of the beautiful Annabel Lee;
And so, all the night-tide, I lie down by the side
Of my darling, my darling, my life and my bride,
In the sepulchre there by the sea—
In her tomb by the sounding.

--Edgar Allan Poe

Discussion Ideas for "Annabel Lee"

1. Why did a wind come and take the maiden away from the narrator?

   a. Their love was too intense, and the angels were envious.
   b. She wanted to die young.
   c. The moon and sun were on a collision course.

2. The maiden's only reason for living was

   a. to enjoy living beside the sea.
   b. to one day be an angel.
   c. to love and be loved by the narrator of this poem.

3. Love poems are usually wrought with intense emotion. But poems about lost or stolen loves are even more intense.

   You can either write about a real or an imaginary lost or stolen love, one which will leave the reader feeling emotionally drained after reading what you have written.

4. How would Edgar Allan Poe's "Annabel Lee" read if the maiden's name were changed to one of these? Read the poem again, but this time, substitute one of the names below in place of Annabel Lee.

   Celeste Henley — Marva-Jean Lincoln
   Abigail Torrence — Lucille Draper

5. Discuss the effect of names on the story line of a poem. How important are names to a story?

6. **Listen** to the poem, "Annabel Lee," as it is read aloud. Do you hear a sound device called **alliteration**—the repetition of the same consonant sound at the beginning of words—to create a musical effect? Discuss how these details of sound contribute to the overall effect of the poem.

7. Does the poem use **figurative** language—words that create images in order to compare one thing to another? Discuss how figurative language contributes to the overall effect of the poem.

8. Write a short report about Edgar Allan Poe. Use encyclopedias, biographies, CD-ROM references, or on-line information services. In your research, find out who Poe wrote about when he created the poem, "Annabel Lee."

I'm Nobody

I'm nobody! Who are you?
Are you nobody, too?
Then there's a pair of us—don't tell!
They'd banish us, you know.

How dreary to be somebody!
How public like a frog
To tell your name the livelong day
To an admiring bog!

--Emily Dickinson

Discussion Ideas for "I'm Nobody"

1. According to the narrator, people who like to toot their own horn

   a. resemble a croaking frog.
   b. sound like passing freight trains.
   c. are a model for others.

2. The type of person the poet celebrates is

   a. anybodies. b. somebodies. c. nobodies.

3. In this poem, Emily Dickinson celebrates those people who are seldom noticed, people who don't crave the limelight.

   This poem is critical of important-feeling people. The second stanza could be rewritten in a number of ways using an equally graphic comparison. Try your hand at rewriting the second stanza so that it will be as compelling as Emily Dickinson's original version.

4. Try writing a companion piece to Emily Dickinson's poem. Instead of "I'm Nobody," title your poem, "I'm Somebody." In other words, do an inversion of the Dickinson poem.

5. **Read** the poem, "I'm Nobody," aloud two times. The first time, **read** for pure enjoyment. The second time, read to analyze and gather details about the meaning. Does the poem use **figurative** language—words that create images in order to compare one thing to another? Discuss how figurative language contributes to the overall effect of the poem.

6. **Find** two important or unusual facts about Emily Dickinson that most others might not know. Share your facts with them. Compile all facts presented into a booklet.

Little Boy Blue

The little toy dog is covered with dust,
But sturdy and staunch he stands;
The little toy soldier is red with rust,
And his musket molds in his hands.
Time was when the little toy dog was new
And the soldier was passing fair;
And that was the time when our Little Boy Blue
Kissed them and put them there.

"Now don't you go till I come," he said,
"And don't you make any noise!"
So toddling off to his trundle bed,
He dreamt of the pretty toys;
And, as he was dreaming, an angel song
Awakened our Little Boy Blue—
Oh! the years are many, the years are long,
But the little toy friends are true!

Ay, faithful to Little Boy Blue they stand,
Each in the same old place,
Awaiting the touch of a little hand,
The smile of a little face;
And they wonder, as waiting the long years through,
In the dust of that little chair,
What has become of our Little Boy Blue
Since he kissed them and put them there.

--Eugene Field

Discussion Ideas for "Little Boy Blue"

1. What one word best describes the way his toy friends felt toward Little Boy Blue?

   a. abandoned
   b. faithful
   c. envious

2. What toys did Little Boy Blue tell to stay where they were until he returned?

   a. a teddy bear and a lion
   b. a truck and a school bus
   c. a soldier and a dog

3. The phrase "kissed them and put them there" is used in the eighth line as well as the twenty-fourth line, but each one evokes a different emotion. What are the differences in the two?

4. Think of some remembrance that someone gave you, which simply collects dust now. Make a list of thoughts that cross your mind every time you see it, forgotten and ignored. Then, take items from your list to pen your own poem of lament.

5. Go through your house and identify objects you have accumulated over the years from friends and family members. Design a Family Tree and an Extended Family Tree based on the objects they have located in china closets and on dresser and mantel tops. Rather than putting names of people on the trees, list the objects. Once you have completed your trees, you can then write a poem that will link the members on one of your trees.

6. **Listen** to the poem, "Little Boy Blue," as it is read aloud two times. The first time, **listen** for pure enjoyment. The second time, **listen** to the sound of the poem as well as its meaning. Do you hear a sound device called **alliteration**—the repetition of the same consonant sound at the beginning of words—to create a musical effect? Discuss how these details of sound contribute to the overall effect of the poem.

A Red, Red Rose

O my Luve's like a red, red rose
That's newly sprung in June:
O my Luve's like the melodie
That's sweetly play'd in tune!

As fair art thou, my bonnie lass,
So deep in luve am I:
And I will luve thee still, my dear,
Till a' the seas gang dry:

Till a' the seas gang dry, my dear,
And the rocks melt wi' the sun;
I will luve thee still, my dear,
While the sands o' life shall run.

And fare thee weel, my only Luve
And fare thee weel awhile!
And I will come again, my Luve,
Tho' it were ten thousand mile.

--Robert Burns

Discussion Ideas for "A Red, Red Rose"

1. How widely separated are the lovers in this poem?

   a. two towns away b. ten thousand miles c. in the neighboring county

2. Which one of these choices does not reflect how long the narrator will love his bonnie lass?

   a. as long as the sands of life shall run
   b. until the earth and sky are one
   c. till all the seas go dry
   d. until the rocks melt with the sun

3. No writing course would be complete without the opportunity to write a love poem. In his celebration of love, Robert Burns likens his love to a "red, red rose/…newly sprung in June" and to a "melodie/…sweetly play'd in tune."

   Love poems, especially, lend themselves to the use of comparisons. Notice the word *like*, which signals the approach of the comparison and intends it in a very literal way. Direct comparisons, signaled by *like* or *as*, are known as similes.

   Consider these lines for starters. Might one of them work as the opening line of your love poem? If so, use it. If not, create your own line.

   My love is like a butterfly
   My love is like a snuggly pig
   My love is like a burning bush
   My love is like a missing tooth
   My love is like gardenia scent
   My love is like a nighttime star
   My love is like a fiery coal
   My love is like a meteorite

4. Notice the many words in this poem that are either spelled differently from words in modern English or that no longer exist in the language. Discuss the modern-day words for these.

   luve melodie thou gang weel

5. What are the actual words for these contractions?

   play'd a' wi' o' tho'

6. What do these contracted forms and archaic words add to the poem? What does the dictionary say about archaic words?

7. **Read** the poem, "A Red, Red Rose," aloud two times. The first time, **read** for pure enjoyment. The second time, read to analyze and gather details about the meaning. Does the poem use **figurative** language—words that create images in order to compare one thing to another? Discuss how figurative language contributes to the overall effect of the poem.

The Rhodora

In May, when sea winds pierced our solitudes,
I found the fresh rhodora in the woods,
Spreading its leafless blooms in a damp nook,
To please the desert and the sluggish brook.
The purple petals, fallen in the pool,
Made the black water with their beauty gay;
Here might the redbird come his plumes to cool,
And court the flower that cheapens his array.
Rhodora! if the sages ask thee why
This charm is wasted on the earth and sky,
Tell them, dear, that if eyes were made for seeing,
Then Beauty is its own excuse for being:
Why thou wert there, O rival of the rose!
I never thought to ask, I never knew;
But, in my simple ignorance, suppose
The selfsame Power that brought me there brought you.

--Ralph Waldo Emerson

Discussion Ideas for "The Rhodora"

1. One of the unusual features of "The Rhodora" is that

   a. it has blossoms but no leaves.
   b. it blooms only every other year.
   c. it looks like a rose.

2. According to the narrator, what is reason enough for the existence of anything?

   a. its beauty
   b. its market value
   c. its popularity

3. Notice the author's use of color images in this poem: purple petals, black water, and redbird. We could expand his technique to employ still more color images. What color words would work with these words?

   ______________________ winds
   ______________________ desert
   ______________________ flower
   ______________________ earth
   ______________________ sky

4. One of the best-known lines in American literature is found in this poem. To quote Emerson: "If eyes were made for seeing, then Beauty is its own excuse for being." If eyes exist for no other purpose than to appreciate the beauty in nature, that is reason enough for having eyes.

   But surely there are other reasons for eyes. Is it possible we could come up with some modern-day variations of the Emerson quotation? For starters, what about this line?

   If eyes were made for seeing, then sirens have no need for being.

   Now, try writing two variations of your own.

5. Find one important or unusual fact about Ralph Waldo Emerson that most others might not know. Share your fact with them. Compile all facts presented into a booklet.

Seth Compton

When I died, the circulating library
Which I built up for Spoon River,
And managed for the good of inquiring minds,
Was sold at auction on the public square,
As if to destroy the last vestige
Of my memory and influence.
For those of you who could not see the virtue
Of knowing Volney's *Ruins* as well as Butler's *Analogy*,
And *Faust* as well as *Evangeline*,
Were really the power in the village,
And often you asked me,
"What is the use of knowing the evil in the world?"
I am out of your way now, Spoon River,
Choose your own good and call it good.
For I could never make you see
That no one knows what is good
Who knows not what is evil;
And no one knows what is true
Who knows not what is false.

--Edgar Lee Masters

Discussion Ideas for "Seth Compton"

1. Why does the narrator think the Spoon River library was sold at public auction?

   a. to destroy his memory
   b. to raise money to build a new firehouse
   c. because nobody in Spoon River could read

2. According to the narrator, "no one knows what is good"

   a. unless he/she is good.
   b. without knowing the worth of evil.
   c. until he/she reaches old age.

3. Use lines 16 and 17 of this poem as a basis for discussing values and creating a values list. See how many pairings of examples you can provide in a list of good and evil. (Try to list at least ten.)

Good	Evil

4. Using lines 18 and 19 as a basis for discussing truth and falsity, try creating another list of pairings. (Try to list at least ten.)

Truths	Falsehoods

5. The tragic tone of this poem is set early, in these lines.

   The circulating library
   Was sold at auction on the public square
   As if to destroy the last vestige
   Of my memory and influence.

   For Seth Compton, what he treasured most was the library he built up for the townspeople in Spoon River. To see it destroyed before his death dealt him a crippling blow.

   What is the legacy left behind by someone you know? What if that legacy went up in smoke? Write a poem that reveals the heartbreak and suffering of that person.

Answer Key

Hoops (page 5)

1. Several things, including the short line lengths, the many one-syllable words, the trochaic rhythms, and the subject matter itself. The poem is as fast-moving as is the game of basketball itself.
2. Both, although we see him primarily in the role of a shooter.
3. The hoops make for points, and they must be defended against the shots of opposing players. If the poem were titled *Oops*, the title would suggest a mistake, something in error.
4. The answers will vary.
5. The answers will vary.

No Right Words (page 7)

1. She doesn't know. It could be for the things he says to her or the way he looks at her. She's not sure.
2. The poem comes full circle in the last line. Together, the first and last line "frame" the poem.
3. The answers will vary.
4. The answers will vary.

Noah's Wife (page 9)

1. The answers will vary.
2. The torrents of rain pound like fire and brimstone on the wooden roof. Notice the specific diction: torrents; the action verb: pound; and the comparison using like.
3. The answers will vary.
4. The answers will vary.

School (page 11)

1. He doesn't dislike school at all. He tells us in the opening stanza that he doesn't view school as an institution of grief.
2. Instead of saying, "School is no fun," the author magnifies the sentiment and says, "is an institution of grief." The place sounds like a prison or sanitarium. There is a rule against chewing gum in school. But "so many...enjoy it" and so does he.
3. Whispering and chewing gum, especially. Today's rules would have to do with drugs and weapons on school premises.
4. The answers will vary.
5. The answers will vary.

Soulstring on the South Wind (page 13)

1. Tomorrow will bring the realization of a dream. The south winds will usher in warm days. The south wind is like a companion to the narrator.
2. The poem moves from the dormancy of winter to things bursting alive in spring—bird's chorales and dancing leaves of trees.
3. There is a oneness between them. They are soulmates.
4. He is either protecting himself from the cold of the north winds, or he is turning his back on them. He is obviously eager for south winds to return.
5. Let students explore this one. Soulmates and soulstrings have an obvious connection.
6. The answers will vary.
7. The answers will vary.
8. The answers will vary.

To My Child (page 15)

1. They are personified here. The capitalization allows the words to bring attention to themselves. They are such memorable moments in the life of her child; they are like time periods: Joy, Sorrow, Laughter, Tears.
2. She experiences mixed emotions. She is glad her child can move on with his/her life and experience "new adventures." But she is sad that all the wonderful memories of the past are history now.
3. The poem contains the component parts of a friendly letter: salutation, body, closing, and signature.
4. The answers will vary.
5. The answers will vary.

The Seasons (page 26)
1. An operetta is a play with both singing and speaking parts.
2. The sky people are mythical fun-loving groups who have been given human qualities. The sky people and earthlings display similar emotions, which include anger, compassion, envy, boastfulness, pity, happiness, etc.
3. The sky people think they are more important than earthlings. They have a superiority complex; therefore, it is even more appropriate that the most important person, the arbitrator, turns out to be not just an earthling, but a child earthling.
4. The answers will vary.
5. The answers will vary.
6. The answers will vary.

Annabel Lee (page 29)
1. a. Their love was too intense, and the angels were envious.
2. c. to love and be loved by the narrator of this poem.
3. The answers will vary.
4. The answers will vary.
5. The answers will vary.
6. Stanza 1—"m" sound/many, maiden, may
   Stanza 3—"k" sound/cloud, kinsman, came
7. Writers often use comparisons as a means of creating word pictures. Similies are the more obvious types of comparisons. They mean literally what they say and are most often signaled by the words <u>like</u> or <u>as</u>. Stanza 2—"He loved with a love that was more than love." Stanza 5—"Our love was stronger by far than the love of those who were older than we."
8. The answers will vary.

I'm Nobody (page 31)
1. a. resemble a croaking frog.
2. c. nobodies.
3. The answers will vary.
4. The answers will vary.
5. Stanza 2—"How dreary to be a somebody! How public like a frog..."
6. The answers will vary.

Little Boy Blue (page 33)
1. b. faithful
2. c. a soldier and a dog
3. The answers will vary.
4. The answers will vary.
5. The answers will vary.
6. Stanza 1—sturdy, staunch, red, rust, musket, molds

A Red, Red Rose (page 35)
1. b. ten thousand miles
2. b. until the earth and sky are one
3. The answers will vary.
4. Love, melody, you, go/going, well
5. Played, all, with, of, through
6. Words that are no longer used in a language—outdated
7. Stanza 1—"O my Luve's like a red, red rose."

The Rhodora (page 37)
1. a. it has blossoms but no leaves.
2. a. its beauty
3. The answers will vary.
4. The answers will vary.
5. The answers will vary.

Seth Compton (page 39)
1. a. to destroy his memory
2. b. without knowing the worth of evil.
3. The answers will vary.
4. The answers will vary.
5. The answers will vary.